ATLANTA FALCONS

BY JOSH ANDERSON

Stride
An Imprint of The Child's World®
childsworld.com

The Child's World
childsworld.com

Published by The Child's World®
800-599-READ • www.childsworld.com

Photography Credits
Cover: © Sarah Stier / Staff / Getty Images; page 1: © Africa Studio / Shutterstock; page 3: © Rob Carr / Staff / Getty Images; page 5: Jared C. Tilton / Staff / Getty Images; page 6: © Mike Powell / Staff / Getty Images; page 9: © Jonathan Bachman / Stringer / Getty Images; page 10: © Kevin C. Cox / Staff / Getty Images; page 11: © stevezmina1 / Getty Images; page 12: © Kevin C. Cox / Staff / Getty Images; page 12: © Sarah Stier / Staff / Getty Images; page 13: © Chris Hill / Shutterstock; page 13: © Kevin C. Cox / Staff / Getty Images; page 14: © Kevin C. Cox / Staff / Getty Images; page 15: © Doug Pensinger / Staff / Getty Images; page 16: © Vernon Biever / Associated Press; page 16: © Todd Kirkland / Stringer / Getty Images; page 17: © Al Golub/ZUMA Press / Newscom; page 17: © Kevin C. Cox / Staff / Getty Images; page 18: © AP / Associated Press; page 18: © Chuck Solomon/ Icon SMI / Newscom; page 19: © Streeter Lecka / Staff / Getty Images; page 19: © Gregory Shamus / Staff / Getty Images; page 20: © Jamie Squire / Staff / Getty Images; page 20: © Kevin C. Cox / Staff / Getty Images; page 21: © Sarah Stier / Staff / Getty Images; page 21: © Kevin Hoffman / Stringer / Getty Images; page 22: © Michael Reaves / Stringer / Getty Images; page 23: © Tom Hauck / Staff / Getty Images; page 23: © stevezmina1 / Getty Images; page 25: © Andy Lyons / Staff / Getty Images; page 26: © Greg Fiume / Stringer / Getty Images; page 29: © Otto Greule Jr / Stringer / Getty Images

ISBN Information
9781503857896 (Reinforced Library Binding)
9781503860391 (Portable Document Format)
9781503861756 (Online Multi-user eBook)
9781503863118 (Electronic Publication)

LCCN 2021952659

Printed in the United States of America

BRINGING THE WORLD TO YOUNG READERS 1968

TABLE OF CONTENTS

GO FALCONS!

The Atlanta Falcons compete in the National Football **League's** (NFL) National Football Conference (NFC). They play in the NFC South **division**, along with the Carolina Panthers, New Orleans Saints, and Tampa Bay Buccaneers. Fans of the team have been lucky in recent years. The Falcons made it to the NFL **playoffs** five times between 2010 and 2017. And they went all the way to the **Super Bowl** after the 2016 season. Let's learn more about the Falcons!

NFC SOUTH DIVISION

Atlanta Falcons

Carolina Panthers

New Orleans Saints

Tampa Bay Buccaneers

CORDARRELLE PATTERSON (RIGHT) TOTALED 1,166 TOTAL YARDS AND 11 TOUCHDOWNS AS A RUSHING AND RECEIVING THREAT IN 2021.

BECOMING THE FALCONS

The Falcons joined the NFL as an **expansion team** in 1966. Originally, they played in the NFL's Eastern Conference. The Falcons had their first winning season in 1971, when they finished with a 7–6–1 record. Their first playoff appearance was in 1978. Although the Falcons have never won the Super Bowl, they have played in it twice. They faced the Denver Broncos in Super Bowl 33. In Super Bowl 51, they played the New England Patriots.

MODERN FOOTBALL HELMETS AND FACE MASKS PROVIDE MORE PROTECTION THAN THOSE USED IN EARLIER YEARS.

BY THE NUMBERS

The Falcons have won **SEVEN** NFC South division titles.

540
points scored by the team in 2016—a Falcons record!

NINE
Falcons enshrined in the Pro Football Hall of Fame

14
wins for the Falcons in 1998

BRIAN HILL (TOP) PLAYED IN 39 GAMES FOR THE FALCONS FROM 2017 TO 2020.

"RISE UP" HAS BEEN THE FALCONS' TEAM SLOGAN SINCE 2010.

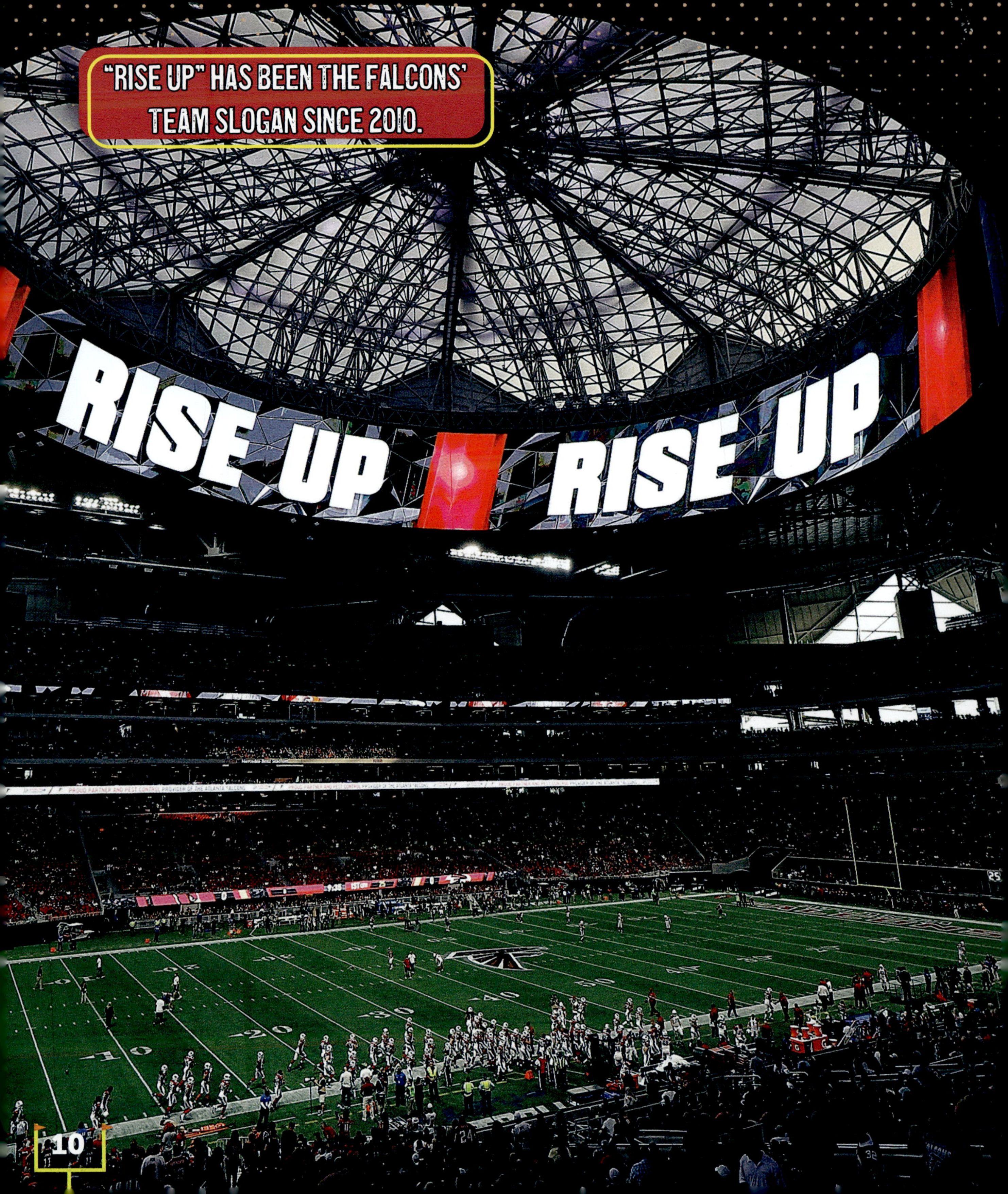

GAME DAY

The Falcons play their home games at Mercedes-Benz **Stadium**. Many fans call it "The Benz." The stadium opened in 2017. Its circular roof is made from eight triangle-shaped pieces that open and close. The roof was designed to look like the wings of a bird when opened. Outside the stadium is a giant falcon statue. On game days, The Benz can hold up to 71,000 fans. The building hosted Super Bowl 53 in 2019.

We're Famous!

The 1991 Falcons adopted a popular song of the time as their anthem. "Too Legit to Quit" by MC Hammer pumped up both players and fans that season. The Falcons finished 10-6 and made the playoffs. And cornerback Deion Sanders and coach Jerry Glanville even had small parts in the song's music video!

UNIFORM

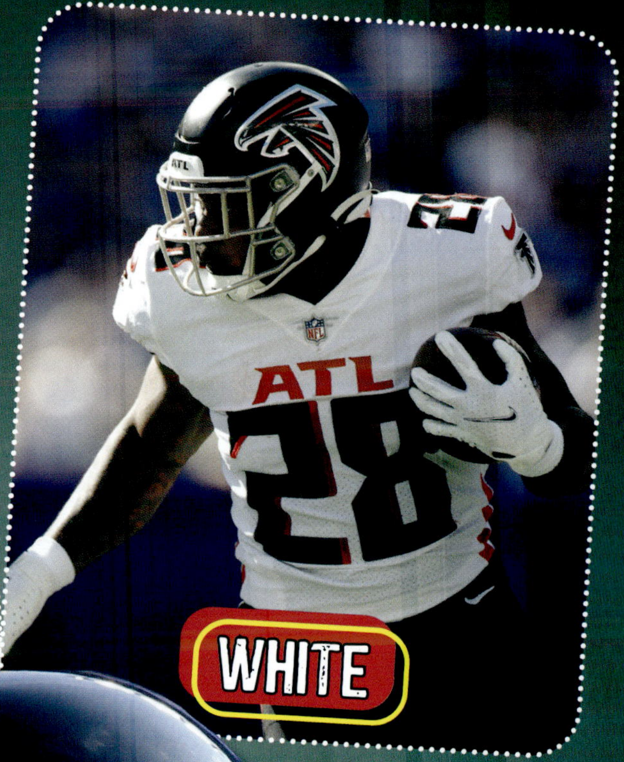

Truly Weird

The Falcons' team mascot once flew the coop! During their early years, the team's mascot was an actual live bird. One day in 1966, as the team was working out on the field, the bird just flew away. Luckily, the bird was found a few days later sitting on top of a food factory 12 miles (19 km) away.

Alternate Jersey

Sometimes teams wear an alternate jersey that is different from their home and away jerseys. It might be a bright color or have a unique theme. The Falcons wore these red and black jerseys for a 2020 game against the Detroit Lions. The new look didn't prove lucky, though. The Falcons lost the game by one point!

WHEN THEY ARE NOT PERFORMING FOR THE CROWD AT GAMES, MEMBERS OF THE ATLANTA FALCONS CHEERLEADERS ATTEND CHARITY EVENTS AND COMMUNITY GATHERINGS THROUGHOUT THE CITY.

TEAM SPIRIT

Going to a game at The Benz can be a blast! One of the most famous ways Falcons fans express their enthusiasm is by doing the "Dirty Bird." The Dirty Bird began as a **touchdown** celebration that was popularized by running back Jamal Anderson in 1998. Some fans and players today still embrace the dance as a symbol of their excitement for the team. The Atlanta Falcons Cheerleaders entertain the crowd at every game. They are joined on the sideline by the team's mascot, Freddie Falcon. He's a huge costumed bird who loves when the Falcons score touchdowns!

HEROES OF HISTORY

Claude Humphrey

Defensive End | 1968–1978

Humphrey was named Defensive **Rookie** of the Year in 1968. Although **sacks** were not kept as an official stat during his career, Humphrey had 99.5 during his time in Atlanta. He was chosen for the **Pro Bowl** six times. Humphrey is a member of the Pro Football Hall of Fame.

Julio Jones

Wide Receiver | 2011–2020

Jones was one of the NFL's top pass catchers during his decade in Atlanta. He led the league in receiving in 2015 and again in 2018. Jones is the Falcons' top receiver of all time, with 848 receptions and 12,896 yards. He was Atlanta's single-season leader for receiving yards for six seasons in a row, from 2014 to 2019. Jones was chosen for the Pro Bowl seven times as a Falcon.

Deion Sanders

Cornerback | 1989–1993

"Neon Deion" Sanders started his long career with the Falcons. He earned three trips to the Pro Bowl during that time. Amazingly, Sanders was a two-sport star! At the same time he played for the Falcons, he played baseball for the New York Yankees and the Atlanta Braves. He even once joined the Braves for a baseball game after playing for the Falcons earlier in the day.

Roddy White

Wide Receiver | 2005–2015

White registered more than 1,000 receiving yards in six straight seasons from 2007 to 2012. He led the league in catches in 2010 with 115. He finished his career with 808 catches, 10,863 receiving yards, and 63 touchdown catches. He was chosen for the Pro Bowl four times.

The Falcons defeat the New York Giants 27–16 for their first victory ever.

In their first playoff game ever, the Falcons defeat the Philadelphia Eagles 14–13.

BIG DAYS

The Falcons defeat the Packers in the NFC Championship Game and advance to Super Bowl 51.

With the fourth overall pick in the 2021 NFL Draft, the Falcons select tight end Kyle Pitts.

MODERN-DAY MARVELS

Grady Jarrett

Defensive Tackle | Debut: 2015

Jarrett tied a Super Bowl record when he recorded three sacks in Super Bowl 51 against the New England Patriots. After compiling 7.5 sacks in 2019, he was selected for his first Pro Bowl. Jarrett followed that up in 2020 when he was selected again.

Deion Jones

Linebacker | Debut: 2016

Jones has five career interceptions returned for a touchdown. That's the most of any player since he entered the league. Jones was selected for the Pro Bowl after the 2017 season, when he had three interceptions and combined for 138 tackles.

Cordarrelle Patterson

Running Back | Debut: 2021

Four-time Pro-Bowler Patterson joined the Falcons in 2021. Before coming to Atlanta, Patterson was known mostly for kick returning. In his career, he has returned eight kickoffs for touchdowns. He holds the NFL record for the longest kickoff return in NFL history. In 2021, he played a big role on offense. Patterson totaled 1,166 combined yards and 11 touchdowns.

Kyle Pitts

Tight End | Debut: 2021

Pitts and the Falcons made history when the team selected him fourth overall in the 2021 NFL Draft. No tight end had ever been selected earlier. The team valued Pitts so highly for his unique mix of speed, strength, and receiving ability. He was selected for the Pro Bowl after his rookie season.

MATT RYAN STARTED MORE THAN 200 GAMES AT QUARTERBACK FOR THE FALCONS.

THE GOAT

GREATEST OF ALL TIME

MATT RYAN

By the end of the 2021 season, Ryan ranked eighth all-time in passing yards and ninth in passing touchdowns. He led the team to the playoffs six times. Ryan was a key player on the Falcons team that reached Super Bowl 51. He was picked as the NFL's **Most Valuable Player** in 2016. He threw 38 touchdown passes that season. Ryan was selected for the Pro Bowl four times.

#1

FAN FAVORITE

Jamal Anderson–Running Back

1994–2001

Anderson danced his way into the hearts of Falcons fans with his "Dirty Bird" touchdown celebration. He rushed for more than 1,000 yards in four of his eight seasons with the team. Anderson was a key part of the 1998 team that advanced to play in Super Bowl 33.

THE BIG GAME

JANUARY 17, 1999 – NFC CHAMPIONSHIP GAME

In more than 30 seasons of play, the Falcons had never advanced to the Super Bowl. The Minnesota Vikings stood in their way of playing in Super Bowl 33. The Vikings had gone 15–1 in the regular season. The game between the two best teams in the NFC was as close as expected. The Falcons trailed by seven with about a minute left. But quarterback Chris Chandler threw a 16-yard touchdown to Terance Mathis to tie the game. In **overtime**, Falcons kicker Morten Andersen hit a 38-yard field goal to send the Falcons to the big game!

TERANCE MATHIS (LEFT) CAUGHT TWO TOUCHDOWNS IN THE NFC CHAMPIONSHIP GAME.

MIKE SMITH LED THE FALCONS TO 66 REGULAR-SEASON WINS AND FIVE PLAYOFF APPEARANCES.

AMAZING FEATS

31 Touchdown Passes

In 1980 by
QUARTERBACK
Steve Bartkowski

1,846 Rushing Yards

In 1998 by
RUNNING BACK
Jamal Anderson

17 Rushing Touchdowns

In 2008 by
RUNNING BACK
Michael Turner

15 Receiving Touchdowns

In 1993 by
WIDE RECEIVER
Andre Rison

ALL-TIME BEST

PASSING YARDS

Matt Ryan
59,735
Steve Bartkowski
23,470
Chris Miller
14,066

RUSHING YARDS

Gerald Riggs
6,631
Michael Turner
6,081
William Andrews
5,986

RECEIVING YARDS

Julio Jones
12,896
Roddy White
10,863
Terance Mathis
7,349

SACKS*

Claude Humphrey
99.5
John Abraham
68.5
John Zook
61

SCORING

Matt Bryant
1,163
Morten Andersen
806
Mick Luckhurst
558

INTERCEPTIONS

Rolland Lawrence
39
Ray Brown
31
Scott Case and Ray Buchanan
30

*unofficial before 1982

RUNNING BACK GERALD RIGGS SCORED 48 TOUCHDOWNS DURING HIS SEVEN SEASONS WITH THE FALCONS.

GLOSSARY

division (dih-VIZSH-un): a group of teams within the NFL that play each other more frequently and compete for the best record

expansion team (EK-span-shun TEEM): a new team added to the league

Hall of Fame (HAHL of FAYM): a museum in Canton, Ohio, that honors the best players in NFL history

league (LEEG): an organization of sports teams that compete against each other

Most Valuable Player (MOHST VAL-yuh-bul PLAY-uhr): a yearly award given to the top player in the NFL

overtime (OH-vuhr-tym): extra time played when teams are tied at the end of four quarters

playoffs (PLAY-ahfs): a series of games played after the regular season that decides which two teams play in the Super Bowl

Pro Bowl (PRO BOWL): the NFL's All-Star Game where the best players in the league compete

rookie (RUH-kee): a player playing in his first season

sack (SAK): when a quarterback is tackled behind the line of scrimmage before he can throw the ball

stadium (STAY-dee-uhm): a building with a field and seats for fans where teams play

Super Bowl (SOO-puhr BOWL): the championship game of the NFL, played between the winners of the AFC and NFC

touchdown (TUTCH-down): a play in which the ball is brought into the other team's end zone, resulting in six points

FIND OUT MORE

IN THE LIBRARY

Bulgar, Beth and Mark Bechtel. *My First Book of Football.* New York, NY: Time Inc. Books, 2015.

Jacobs, Greg. *The Everything Kids' Football Book, 7th Edition*. Avon, MA: Adams Media, 2021.

Sports Illustrated Kids. *The Greatest Football Teams of All Time*. New York, NY: Time Inc. Books, 2018.

Wyner, Zach. *Atlanta Falcons*. New York, NY: AV2 Books, 2020.

ON THE WEB

Visit our website for links about the Atlanta Falcons:
childsworld.com/links

Note to parents, teachers, and librarians: We routinely verify our web links to make sure they are safe and active sites. Encourage your readers to check them out!

INDEX

ABOUT THE AUTHOR

Josh Anderson has published over 50 books for children and young adults. His two boys are the greatest joys in his life. Hobbies include coaching his sons in youth basketball, no-holds-barred games of Apples to Apples, and taking long family walks. His favorite NFL team is a secret he'll never share!